Hey,

Where's that BUG?

Look inside, silly, and then you can
stop bugging me.

PUBLISHING INFO

Published by Romney Fine Art & Publications LLC
P. O. Box 1533
McCall, Idaho   83638

Printed in China
First Printing March 2008

Publisher's Cataloging-In-Publication Data
(Prepared by The Donohue Group, Inc.)

Romney, Mary Anne.
  Where's that bug? : the big adventure story book / by author, photographer and artist Mary Anne Romney.

    p. : col. ill. ; cm.

  Interest age level: 005-011.
  ISBN: 978-0-9816825-0-1

1. Insects--Juvenile literature. 2. Insects. 1. Title.

QL467.2 .R66 2008
595.7

ෆෆෆෆෆෆෆෆෆෆ

Thank you
for dragon
me into this
book,
Bug Lady.

Where's that BUG?

The BIG ADVENTURE STORY BOOK

by Author, Photographer and Artist

Mary Anne Romney

Bugs? Where? I love bugs. Bugs are so pretty. Tra la la la la.

Hey you guys, look who bugged somebody!

Come bug *me*. I know what to do with bugs.....

ACKNOWLEDGEMENT

To McKenna, for bugging me about getting this book out to kids like you.

To my children, their wives and kids.....because all of you love me despite how much I bug you.

To Shane because you always said I could do it and wouldn't stop bugging me until I did.

To my Dad, who always loved me no matter how much I drove him buggie.

To my Heavenly Father, whose kindly patience helped me turn from a caterpillar with potential into a vivid butterfly in flight.

Most of all, to my sweetheart, Rick, for your unending support, kindness and encouragement without bugging me a whole lot.

ෲෲෲෲෲෲ

Table of Contents

This book may really
bug you.

If it doesn't, I will.

Chapter One: **The Adventure** . . . 1

Chapter Two: **Outerspacemen and Princesses** . . . 9

Chapter Three: **A Spider Takes a Drink** . . . 25

Chapter Four: **Lunch in the Meadow** . . . 43

Chapter Five: **Sleepy Time** . . . 61

Cool Things About Nature Club . . . 72

For Parents . . . 73

The BUG Lady . . . 74

The Adventure

Hello! My name is Mary Anne, but most of my friends call me **"The Bug Lady"**. They call me that because of the adventure I had this summer finding out all about bugs.

It was an accident, you see. I love to take pictures and that's what I was doing. I got a new digital camera for Christmas and since then I love to go all over the place and take pictures of everything that I see. Do you have a camera? It's a lot of fun and I hope you get to try it.

I live in the mountains. Where do you live? I hope you'll write and tell me.

Oops, back to my story. This is what happened. One day I was taking pictures of the wild flowers that grow here. They are very pretty.

They look like this:

I thought that was pretty fun. Then I found out how to take part of the same flowers and make them look very, very big.

Don't you think that's incredible?

How cool! You can tell everything about what the flower is like, can't you? Here's another one to show you what I mean. First little, then big, ok?

Isn't that amazing?

Pretty soon I was taking walks and taking pictures and practicing getting flowers so that I could see what they are really like when you look very, very closely at them. Wow, was I in for a **BIG** surprise!!!

I was driving down the road and saw some of my favorite flowers. They are called **Indian Blanket Flowers** because they have bright yellow and red colors, just like the blankets that Indians sometimes make. I decided to take pictures of these flowers and see what they looked like if I made their little parts look very big.

Would you like to see what happened?

"Absolutely", says the lovely McKenna.

OK.

Look at the pictures and see if you can discover the surprise.

Am I bugging you yet?

Look closely. What can you see?

Did you guess?

There are **BUGS** in the flowers!

I didn't even see the bugs when I took the pictures, but there they were—looking back at me.

Aren't the colors beautiful? Did you see their stripes? Did you see the pollen on their fuzzy bodies?

You probably think that these bugs are **Honey Bees**. Some are. Some are not. The **Blue Cuckoo Wasp** on these pages is so different. Besides the bright turquoise color, it can't sting you. If you pick it up it will just roll into a little ball.

Seeing these bugs up close made me curious. I decided I wanted to learn more about bugs. I wanted to see what other bugs were hiding in other flowers.

Are you curious, too?

Chapter Two

Outerspace Men and Princesses

The very next day I decided to take a walk down by the Big Pond on my neighbor's farm. I thought it might be a pretty good place to find bugs.

It was a very hot day. I wasn't quite sure where to start. My feet seemed to want to go everywhere at once. Do your feet do that?

I saw a lot of things flying around me, but they were going very, very fast and it was hard to tell what they were. At least I had found some bugs! I decided to sit down by the pond and wait. I wasn't sure what I was waiting for, but my heart began to pound and I felt like something exciting was about to happen.

I held very, very, very still.

Suddenly, something really big began moving towards me. "Wait a minute", I said to myself. "I came here to see little bugs."

"Wow", I thought in my mind as something quite different stopped and looked at me with very bright eyes.

Aren't they just incredible?

"I may not have a picture of bugs yet, but I found something that eats the bugs," I laughed to myself. These birds are called **Sandhill Cranes**.

Just then I looked over my shoulder. Right there on a reed by the pond was the weirdest looking bug. I lifted my camera and pointed right at it; moved the switch in to make it a close-up and......clicked the button. I couldn't believe it. It looked just like an outer space man. There he was......right across from my own house! Do you think he looks like an outer space man?

You will find out when you look closely at bugs that they can really look very interesting, just like this one. This kind of bug is called a **Dragonfly.** Dragonflies are so wonderful. They look like people looking back at you.

There are red ones and blue ones and green ones and gold ones. Some are very tiny. Some are much larger. Some have every color in the rainbow and golden wings. They have fuzzy bodies, too.

Dragonflies like to rest on plants or sticks or branches. Each different kind holds their wings a different way when they hold still. Some hang from the stick with their tails down and wings out. Some rest on top of a stick and put their wings over their face with their tails straight out. Some look like princesses ready for the ball with their glittering wings folded around them.

Dragonflies really like to sit in the sunshine. Do you ever sit in the sunshine on a nice day?

Would you like to see some of the different dragonflies that I found?

This is a picture of my first "outer space man". I had never seen a dragon-fly up close before. This really made me start to get curious. See how he likes his tail pointing down?

It seems like he is floating in space, doesn't it?

This fellow likes to rest with his wings up around him. Would you like to have wings like this and fly away?

Bzzzzzzz.
Whirrrrrrr

I would.

13

This dragonfly has rested so long that a tiny spider has spun a web from his tail across to another branch.

Can you see it?

I call this one Clown Face. What do you think? The part that looks like a mask is really just the bottom part of this dragonfly's face. Can you see the big brown bumps just above the clown "face"? Those are the eyes.

What a crazy looking bug!

Are you reaching for the sun, pretty Red Princess?

Take us with you!

16

See her tiny crown and golden cape?   It's easy to pretend she is a true Princess. Perhaps she lives in a palace of sunshine.

Isn't that fun?

17

Dragonflies are very good at hiding. Many of them are so tiny you have to look closely to see them. Let's play a game. How about the **Where's that BUG?** game? Look at this picture and see if you can tell me where the bug is. Look closely. Remember, it's trying to hide from you. It wants to be invisible. But it's there.

Can you find the bug?

There she is! What a good hiding place. This dragonfly is just the size of the tiny seedpod in this picture. An excellent hiding place!

Don't you think so?

19

Let's play the **Where's that BUG?** game again. See the
picture down below? There's a bug hiding there.

Can you see him?

Where's that BUG? *There's* that bug! You found it!

Smart kid!

Very good.

A lot of bugs stay alive by seeming to be invisible. They hide by wearing a disguise. They camouflage themselves.

Some bugs are the same color as what they live on. Some are the color of leaves or bark or flowers.

Some bugs land very quietly and stay still waiting for other bugs to come along so they can eat them.

Have you ever tried to be invisible by trying to be quiet? I used to hide under the piano as still as a mouse. That was lots of fun.

Do you like to play Hide and Seek?

 **Me, too!**

**Slippery
leaves
catch
drops
of
water.**

**Sometimes
the
drops
roll
off
and
fall
to
the
ground.**

31

Plants with hair catch a lot more water. They catch so much water that they make little bug swimming pools!

It's important to know how plants hold water because then you can learn how bugs take drinks.

Did you ever wonder about that?

Hey, I know what....
Let's follow along and watch a spider take a drink!

Do you want to see?

Spiders use their pedipalps to explore things. A pedipalp looks like a funny extra hand, but it's different. The pedipalps are covered with tiny little hairs. The spider can catch water with these tiny hairs. Did you ever cup your hands and use them to hold water? It's a little like that. The pedipalps look like big claws on a boy spider. On a girl spider they are much smaller.

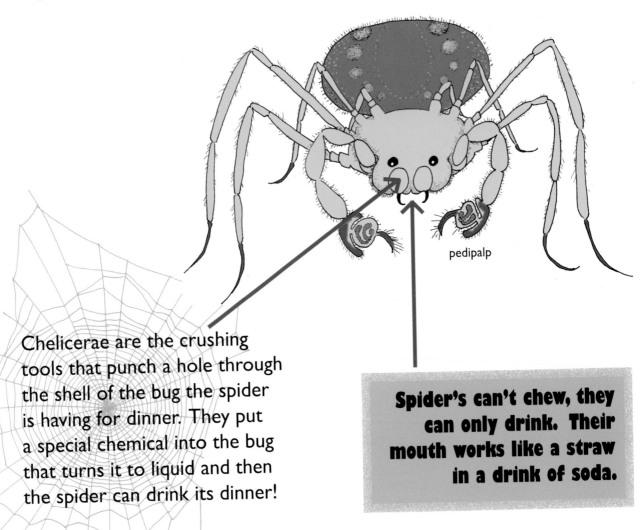

pedipalp

Chelicerae are the crushing tools that punch a hole through the shell of the bug the spider is having for dinner. They put a special chemical into the bug that turns it to liquid and then the spider can drink its dinner!

Spider's can't chew, they can only drink. Their mouth works like a straw in a drink of soda.

I think that this spider sees a nice drop of water and decides to stop for a drink. Scientists are not yet sure exactly how a spider drinks. That's what's fun about taking pictures—sometimes you see things that even scientists haven't seen. You get to decide what you are seeing. You can learn all kinds of wonderful things!

How fun!

Here the spider lowers one of his pedipalps. It looks to me like he's soaking up water from a drop with the tiny, fine hairs.

No rain for a very long time means the spider doesn't get enough water from his food. That is when a spider will take a drink!

See the spider lower his pedipalp and then raise it to his mouth? Do you think he's taking a drink?

Perhaps he is.

Now—off he goes for more exploring!

Wasn't that fun?

Say, do you want to play the **Where's that BUG?** game again? Try this one.

Can you find this very tiny Crab Spider?

No fair?

I know this one was super tough! This spider makes sure it's hard to see. That's how it hunts, catches its food and stays alive. Let's look at it big, ok?

Here's our little friend!

Just because he's tiny, he still knows you're there. If he feels you move or feels the laser light from your camera focus he will run fast to the other side of the flower. He'll be very hard to catch once he knows you're watching him!

Chapter Four

Lunch in the Meadow

Tra la la
dee da.
O happy day!

One day I thought it would be nice to eat my lunch in the meadow. It's a magical place and I love to go there. It always makes me happy inside.

After enjoying my picnic, I rolled over on my tummy and closed my eyes for a nap in the sunshine. A few minutes later, I felt something tickle my nose and opened my eyes. Someone was looking back at me.

Did you ever look a butterfly right in the face?

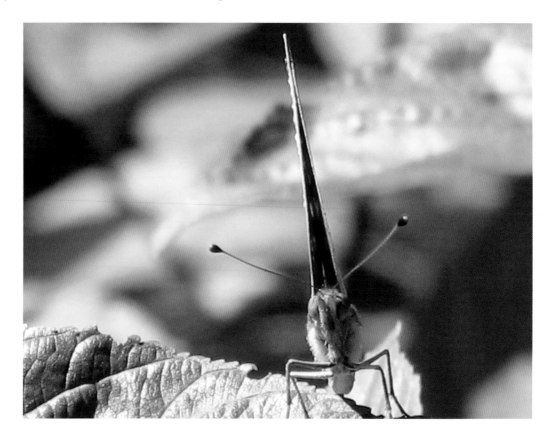

Say "hello" to this playful **Hydaspe Fritillary**. Isn't that a beautiful name for a butterfly? She is at the end of her life. You can tell because she has flown so much that her wing is torn. She has just finished laying her eggs so that her caterpillar children will hatch.

Hello, Momma Butterfly.

I rubbed my nose from the butterfly tickle, then rolled over the other way. Oh, something so small and so beautiful was there on the grass. I took a picture with my camera and made it big so that you can see the incredible colors of this **Green Lacewing**.

Can you imagine why they named it that?

45

As I started to walk around the meadow, I saw some other bugs. This fuzzy **Caterpillar** was chomping on a juicy leaf. I noticed that the caterpillar sometimes hangs upside down while he eats. Can you eat upside down?

Did you know that some bugs eat plants?

Not far from the caterpillar, I saw this bright, red **Convergent Lady Bug.** She finds the **Aphids** quite tasty and there are plenty for her picnic on this **Milkweed** plant.

Like this lady bug, some bugs eat other bugs. You also saw how some bugs eat different parts of plants. They can eat green leaves and stems that are fresh and juicy. They can eat the dead, brown bits of leaves or grass or rotting wood after the plants die. Some bugs especially like that! When bugs eat the dead plants it helps so much to clean up everything that falls to the forest floor or down under the grass in the meadow.

Sometimes I like to lift up rocks or pull apart rotten logs to watch the bugs have their dinner.

There's something else that a lot of bugs eat that we haven't talked about. There is a lot of it in the world and sometimes it makes people sneeze!

    What else do bugs eat?

Bugs just love pollen!

Look at the middle of this flower.

See the little curly anthers dancing on top of the tall filaments? This is a boy or a "male" part of a flower.

Did you know that there are boy and girl parts to flowers?

This is the part of the flower that makes pollen.

Powdery pollen falls from the curly anthers onto the stigma in the center of the rose. The stigma is sticky. This way **Honey Bees** can have lots of pollen but the rose keeps what it needs to make new rose plants. After the petals die, "rose hips" begin to grow under the dead flower. Rose hips are little round balls. They turn orange and red just like autumn leaves do when it becomes cooler in the autumn air.

In a rose, both the male and female parts of the flower are there together. Some flowers have just male parts. Some have just female parts. A flower with both male and female parts is called "perfect".

Isn't that perfectly wonderful?

Some bugs hide in the flowers and wait to catch a bee for dinner. This **Flower Crab Spider** can change colors to match the flower it's on. On the rose it chooses white. On the seed head of a yellow flower it becomes yellow. Can you see it? It's a teensy spider to catch a bee, but the bee doesn't see it coming because the spider matches the rose so well. The spider's strong pedipalps and venom can kill the bee even though it is larger than the spider.

Did I mention that some other guests came to my picnic? This is a **Golden Paper Wasp**. I believe she enjoyed the cantaloupe as much as I did!

Wasps chew up their food and turn it into something like paper to make their nests.

This is a **Yellow Jacket**. Both of these wasps have a horrible sting, so leave them alone while they eat, please.

It's safe to watch from far away!

Here's a most unusual guest! This is a **Lepturine**. Isn't that a fancy name for a fancy bug? Lepturines just love the pollen and nectar in flowers. Why don't you be a Lepturine on next Halloween? That would be so funny! I'd like to see that!

Will you send me a picture?

53

This **Digger Bee** was eating in the meadow, too. He looked like he was eating a piece of corn on the cob. He would take each petal of the thistle flower and comb it from bottom to top with his antennae and pinchers. It made his head bob back and forth.

I was using my laser light to get a good focus on him when suddenly the bee felt the light and turned around to glare at me! He was really mad!!! The pollen on the hair around his mouth looked just like big snarling fangs.

I was so startled that I yelled, "eeek" and jumped. Luckily, I snapped his photograph at the same time!

Buzzzzzz off,
Bug Lady

Would you like to see my angry bee?

Wow! You can see why I think this bee has such an angry face! Do you get mad sometimes?

Do you get an angry face, too?

Bee nice now!

Isn't he ferocious?

55

Thank you for sharing the meadow together with me. Now it's time for the **Where's that BUG?** game. This bug was definitely having a picnic at the same time I was having lunch! In fact, it just about never stops eating. It eats and eats and eats from the second it is born until it turns into a butterfly.

Can you guess what it is?
Can you find the bug?

Good job!

Here is the always eating bug.

This is a caterpillar on the edge of the meadow. I think a bird would have a hard time finding him. Don't you?

57

I love all the fuzzy hair. It helps birds that eat caterpillars grab the hair and miss the bug!

Chomp.
Chomp.

Pretty smart bug.

58

Try this **Where's that BUG?** game if you dare! It is very, very tough. Remember we talked about rose hips? They hold the seeds for roses. This bunch turned red in the cool fall air. Certain teensy tiny bugs are living on them. Need some help?

Let me show you...

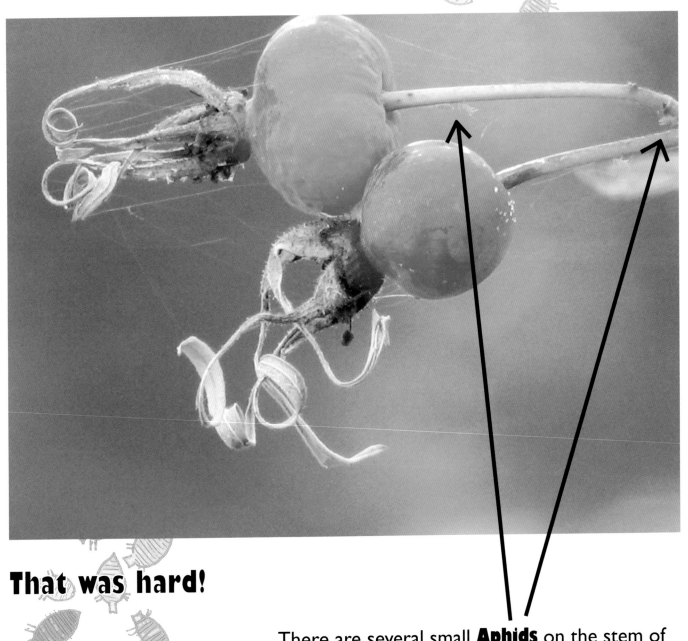

That was hard!

There are several small **Aphids** on the stem of this rose hip. They are the favorite food of Lady Bugs and many other insects.

Chapter Five

Sleepy Time

All summer long I tried to take a picture of a grasshopper. The only problem—they just wouldn't hold still for a second! Are you like that sometimes? One day I decided to go play with my two good friends, McKenna and Hudson. We decided to catch grasshoppers. I like to let Hudson catch mine. He's really good at it. Here are McKenna and Hudson, her little brother, and their three-legged dog, Brit, looking for grasshoppers. We have so much fun!

Hudson catches a bug but it gets away. Too bad, Hudson. Then McKenna catches a nice, tickly grasshopper.

Do you see it?

It's time for me to go. On my way home I wonder if I should give up trying to catch a grasshopper with my camera. I'm so sad. "I know", I say in my mind, "I'll play a game. I'll take pictures of the weeds by the side of the road and just see what bugs are still there this late in the autumn." I start snapping photos.

The sun is almost down and everything is golden. Do you like the golden time of day?

Hey, wait, "What am I seeing?" I ask myself. "Why, it's **Grasshoppers**. I found grasshoppers!" and I start jumping up and down just like I am one. Unbelievable! Incredible! They are all holding still. Why?

I discover the perfect secret about finding bugs that move around a lot. At the golden time of day, just before the sun goes down, bugs tuck themselves into "beds" for the night. They stop wiggling and they rest here and there.....in the little places between a leaf and a stem.....upside down.....sideways....every way!

Silly, sleepy grasshoppers.

I imagine they are all in their pajamas listening to good night stories while it's still a warm autumn night.

Aren't they funny?

Summer has gone by so fast. I'll miss it a lot. It's ok, though, because with my camera, I can still see autumn all year long! I especially love the golden color of aspen trees here in the mountains.

Can you understand why I love them so?

Now that the trees are going to sleep, the bugs are going to sleep, too. They will crawl under a leaf or down in the ground or inside a tree and they will wait.

They will wait like you and I must wait.

Good night, bugs!

Good night, my friends!

Soon the snow and ice will melt and little green plants will shoot up out of the ground looking for the sun. That's when I'll see you again on our....

......next adventure.

With love,

The BUG Lady

Shall we play the **Where's that BUG?** game again before we go? Here's an easy one...

Bug Lady, Lady Bug,
it's all the same to
us!

Where's this bug?

Here is the magnificent **Convergent Lady Bug**. That fancy name means that she has a particular pattern of spots that are different from other Lady Bugs.

Isn't she just beautiful?

Now for the last game today. How about a really hard **Where's that BUG?** game? To get this one, you will have to remember that bugs like to hide by being the same color as the things around them.

You can do it!

Hop to it!

There's the little rascal. What a hard grasshopper to find!

We found you, little grasshopper!

That makes us hopping mad!!!

We'll jump at the chance to see you next time!

Hi. I'm McKenna.

I wanted to tell you about the club **The Bug Lady** and I started this summer. It's the

Cool Things About Nature Club.

Anyone can join for **FREE** and there are a lot of fun things that you can see and do.

You can share the pictures you take of bugs or other interesting things. You can write about your adventures. You can share ideas and ask questions. There are neat T-shirts like, "You're BUGging me!" and "Let's go BUG somebody!" There are posters of the bugs you see in the **Where's That BUG?** book. The **Where's that BUG? Coloring Book** is there and you'll find out about new books as they're ready.

It's really fun to live up here with **The Bug Lady**. Since I'm so lucky, I asked her if I could help share this fun stuff with other kids. Ask your parents if you can check out our web site at:

Thanks, McKenna.

wheresthatbug.com

FOR PARENTS

Hello, folks. Just wanted to let you know a couple of things to get the most out of **Where's that BUG?**. Hmmmm, let's see. Well, first of all please have a chat with your child and make sure they know dangerous bugs to watch out for such as Black Widow, Hobo, Brown Recluse spiders. Encourage your child to observe rather than capture unless you have trained them for safety.

That brings me to the second part. Consider getting a camera and letting them take photos instead. The secret to great bug photos is standing about four or five feet back and zooming in. The bugs don't notice you as much and you get stung a lot less!

As I'm certain you realize, **Where's that BUG?** and/or the author (that would be me) do not take any responsibility for injury or harm as a result of reading this book. It is intended as educational only and requires adult supervision for children.

In case you are interested, the camera I used is more affordable than you might think. I used a **Canon S2 IS**. I highly recommend it. No accessories are necessary as everything your child needs is already there with the technique mentioned above. This camera allows a 48X zoom which is really spiffy.

Please feel free to visit the wheresthatbug.com website for free information that will help your child to become really curious about nature.

Mary Anne Romney is an accomplished author, artist and photographer. Her love of nature and helping it to become cherished by children is a driving force in her life.

Books for kids include the ongoing **Where's that BUG?** series of nature adventures, the **House of Order** spiritual books for teaching kids about being organized, **Fasting for Kids** and other "growing up great" topics.

Books for adults include **Pathway**, original photography and stunning graphic art complement inspirational stories which are based on real life experiences in this unusual series and the **Soul Repair** books, designed to instruct us in the use of the subconscious mind in order to "change and make it stick".

When she isn't writing, you'll find Mary Anne walking in her beloved mountains or catching fish for supper in the local lakes and streams around McCall, Idaho. One thing is certain, Mary Anne always has her camera in hand. That way if there aren't any fish biting, she'll still "catch something"!

Be sure to check out these great websites for books and fine art by Mary Anne:

www.wheresthatbug.com
www.romneyfineartandpublications.com
www.soulrepair.com

CONTACT

Count me in.

You may write to me at:

Mary Anne Romney
The Bug Lady
P. O. Box 1533
McCall, Idaho 83638

or blog me at www.wheresthatbug.com

Doin' anything?

No. Let's go BUG somebody.

Hey, don't leaf me out
you guys!